THE GROVE OF THE EUMENIDES

Tomas Venclova was born in Klaipeda, Lithuania in 1937. From 1956 on Venclova took part in the Lithuanian and Soviet dissident movements, making friends with Natalia Gorbanevskaya and Lyudmila Alexeyeva and other members of the literary and human rights underground. He made his living by translating Baudelaire, Saint-John Perse, T.S. Eliot, Dylan Thomas, W.H. Auden, Robert Frost, Anna Akhmatova, Osip Mandelstam and many others into Lithuanian. Venclova was one of the five founding members of the Lithuanian Helsinki Group, and in 1977 he was forced to emigrate. He taught Russian and Polish literature, as well as Lithuanian language, at Yale University.

Considered one of the major figures of world poetry, his work has been translated by Czesław Miłosz into Polish and by Joseph Brodsky into Russian. His published works include volumes of poetry, criticism, literary biography, conversations and works on Vilnius. He has been the recipient of numerous awards including the Lithuanian National Prize in 2000, the 2002 Prize of Two Nations, which he received jointly with Czesław Miłosz, the 2005 Jotvingiai Prize, the 2005 New Culture of New Europe Prize, and the 2023 Zbigniew Herbert International Literary Award. He holds a number of honorary doctorates and was chosen for Poland's Borderland Award (2001). Venclova's poetry has been translated into more than 20 languages, including Hebrew, Chinese and Albanian, among others. He is active in the contemporary cultural life of Lithuania and continues his democratic work.

His books in English include: *Magnetic North: Conversations with Tomas Venclova* (University of Rochester Press and Boydell & Brewer 2017); *The Junction: Selected Poems*, ed. Ellen Hinsey, tr. Ellen Hinsey, Constantine Rusanov and Diana Senechal (Bloodaxe Books, 2008); *Aleksander Wat: Life and Art of an Iconoclast* (Yale University Press, 1996); *Forms of Hope* (Essays, Sheep Meadow Press, 1999); and *Winter Dialogue*, tr. Diana Senechal (Northwestern University Press, 1997).

For biographical notes on the translators, please see page 119.

TOMAS VENCLOVA

The Grove
OF THE
Eumenides

NEW & SELECTED POEMS

edited by
ELLEN HINSEY

translated by
ELLEN HINSEY
DIANA SENECHAL
RIMAS UŽGIRIS

BLOODAXE BOOKS

ISBN: 978 1 78037 759 9

First published 2025 by
Bloodaxe Books Ltd,
Eastburn,
South Park,
Hexham,
Northumberland NE46 1BS.

www.bloodaxebooks.com
For further information about Bloodaxe titles
please visit our website and join our mailing list
or write to the above address for a catalogue.

Supported using public funding by
**ARTS COUNCIL
ENGLAND**

Cover design: Neil Astley & Pamela Robertson-Pearce.

Printed in Great Britain by Bell & Bain Limited, 303 Burnfield Road,
Thornliebank, Glasgow G46 7UQ, Scotland, on acid-free paper
sourced from mills with FSC chain of custody certification.

L|**C**|**I** Lithuanian
Culture
Institute

The publication of this book has been
financed by the Lithuanian Cultural Institute
in respect of translation costs.
We wish to thank LCI for their support.

ACKNOWLEDGEMENTS

Acknowledgements are due to the following publications in which some of these poems have previously appeared or are forthcoming:

'On Both Sides of Alnas Lake' (*LA Review of Books*);
'To Master Radovan' (*The New England Review*);
'Dictator' (*The New England Review*);
'The Process of Beatification' (*Modern Poetry in Translation*);
'Before the Fort' (*LA Review of Books*);
'Azovstal' (*The Irish Times*);
'The Grove of the Eumenides' (*Vilnius Review*);
'South of the Prospect' (*Modern Poetry in Translation*);
'Landscape with Polyphemus' (*Two Lines*);
'Extra Urbem' (*The New England Review*);
'Caligula at the Gates' (*The Irish Times*);
'August Elegy' (*Asymptote*);
'Notes on Xenophon' (*AGNI*);
'Death of the Argonaut' (*Blue Unicorn*);
'From the Future' (*AGNI*);
'Eos' (*Asymptote*);
'Hurricane' (*Two Lines*);
'Three O'Clock at Night on the Sea' (*POEM*);
'Leaving the Subway with a Pack on My Back' (*Two Lines*);
'The Way to Planty Park, Kraków' (*Vilnius Review*);
'Variation on the Theme of Awakening', 'Syllabic Stanzas'
   (*Four Way Review*);
'Prehistory', 'Three Imperfect Sonnets' (*Asymptote*);
'Prehistory' was republished on *Poetry Daily*.

'Notes on Xenophon' (*AGNI*) and 'From the Future' (*AGNI*), translated by Diana Senechal, were longlisted for Deep Vellum's *Best Literary Translations 2025*. 'Let the Time You No Longer Remember' and a number of other poems appeared in the film *Decadent No. 2419* by Saimir Bajo (2022). A full list of publication sources appears at the end of this book.

CONTENTS

SELECTED WORKS BY TOMAS VENCLOVA

WORKS IN ENGLISH

Magnetic North: Conversations with Tomas Venclova

Vilnius: A Personal History

The Junction: Selected Poems of Tomas Venclova

Poems

Vilnius: A Guide

Forms of Hope (Essays)

Winter Dialogue (Poems)

Aleksander Wat: Life and Art of an Iconoclast

Lithuanian Literature

For a full bibliography of books written in
Lithuanian, English and Russian see page 115.

.

THE GROVE OF THE EUMENIDES

TOMAS VENCLOVA:
Poetry of Witness and The Return of History
by ELLEN HINSEY

In the sixth book of Polybius's *Histories* we find the Greek historian's theory of *anacyclosis*, or the cyclical process of constitutional change. Polybius, who was held hostage in Rome for seventeen years, had ample time to reflect on the process by which societies pass from the heights of the "best" forms of government, such as democracy, to self-destruction through moral decay, transforming themselves into tyrannies or mob rule. But for Polybius, it was not enough to understand this process in general terms. Rather, the historian set out 'by careful observation' to deduce 'the natural origin, genesis, and decadence of […] several forms of government'. It was Polybius's mission, building on earlier classical thought, to leave for us a historian's insights into cycles of governance, including their apexes and nadirs. Again, these were far from theoretical musings, as it is also from Polybius that we have a first-person account of not only the destruction of the Greek city-state of Corinth, but also that of one of the greatest cities of the classical world – the razing of Carthage.

As we well know, the rise and fall of empires is not something unique to the ancient world. And it has been the particular destiny of the poet, essayist and historian Tomas Venclova to have, 'by careful observation', witnessed and chronicled some of the reversals of empires and major changes in Europe over the last eighty years. Born in 1937 in Lithuania, Venclova experienced first-hand the Second World War in Kaunas, with its successive Soviet and German occupations, as well as the postwar imposition of Soviet totalitarianism. He came of age in the early fifties under the tyranny of Stalin's regime as it tightened its grip across Eastern and Central Europe. Early on the poet fell out with the authorities, having understood, after the 1956 suppression of the Hungarian Revolution, the nature of Soviet power. As Venclova's views became known, he was barred from publishing his work. To earn a living, he translated writers such as T.S. Eliot, W.H. Auden, Dylan Thomas, Charles Baudelaire and Osip Mandelstam into Lithuanian. To escape the stifling atmosphere of late communism he travelled extensively throughout the USSR, making the acquaintance of the great Silver Age Russian poets Anna Akhmatova and Boris Pasternak, as well as the younger generation of poets, including Natalya Gorbanevskaya and Joseph Brodsky. His involvement in the seventies with dissident politics and culture, and above all his work as a founding member of the Lithuanian Helsinki Group, led to his expulsion and forced exile in the West, and the stripping of his Soviet citizenship in 1977.

In *The Junction* (Bloodaxe Books, 2009), Venclova's first volume of selected poems in English, we find allusions to many of these experiences, as well as memories of others of his generation, some of whom, still in the USSR or in exile abroad, did not live to see the fall of the Soviet empire. At moments in *The Junction*, we even see cautious flashes of hope for the new beginning it seemed Europe had embarked upon after 1989. In the decade and a half since the book's publication, however, the West has witnessed a series of profound and disquieting shifts that call to mind Polybius's reflections on the cyclical nature of governance. If in 1992 Francis Fukuyama could famously declare 'the end of history' – by which he meant that, for a time, liberal democracy was the order of the day – the new century's first decades have, conversely, brought with them reversals of freedoms, and we have witnessed shadowy descents into tyranny.

For regretfully, as Venclova explores in this new volume, the end of History did not turn out to be the case. Rather, History was merely biding its time – and preparing its return.

The poems in this new selected volume, *The Grove of the*

Eumenides, take up chronologically from where *The Junction* left off, and continue to be characterised by Venclova's authoritative poetic voice, intellectual rigour and ethical discernment. For throughout the last three decades since the fall of the Berlin Wall, Venclova, now in his eighty-eighth year, has remained one of Europe's most powerful and insightful writers. With a poetic gift that is unique in our time – a 'rebellious classicism' – he has described in verse, essays and public addresses the early warning signs, shifts and approaching dangers – but also the resources we have at our disposal for endurance.

Venclova, who recently completed a two-volume history of Lithuania, frequently draws on personal reminiscences, historical memory as well as shared cultural myth. For him, History is never past, but part of a single, living, dynamic tapestry, whose surface vividly glows with events that occurred in 400 BCE or 1945 CE. In his astounding poem 'Flight', included in the present volume, the poet observes space and the passage of time literally and metaphorically from a great height – as he looks out over the vestiges of stone-age geological deposits and the surface of the sweeping tundra, to scars on the landscape left by trenches, concentration camps and the iron curtain, to other traces of the killing sites of the twentieth century – up until our current moment. He knows that as individuals we enter history 'in the middle of events' and are only a tiny incident in their immense flow:

> Your coordinates are between Cap Farewell and the Hebrides,
> or perhaps between your era's polar points – its end and its beginning.
> Continents, oceans and epochs overlap – one upon the other.
> In the realm of Oceanus's sister Mnemosyne – as if on a
> seat-back screen – you observe the far north's tundras and ridges,
> the desolate steppes, the vast deltas of cold rivers – an *oikumene*
> destined for that time's generations.
> Then slowly, you reinvestigate old spectacles: chains of
> trenches, artillery shells searing overhead, the words *Jedem das*

Seine, and the unbreachable concrete walls behind which one couldn't make out prisons, streets, States.

Human beings cannot choose their time or place. But they can choose their fate.

[tr. Ellen Hinsey]

It is perhaps this spirit of expansive reflection – from the classical to the present – that in part characterises the present volume, with poems taken from his recent Lithuanian volumes *Beyond St Anne's and the Bernardines* and *The Grove of the Eumenides*, as well as a few earlier poems from his *Collected Poems* not previously translated.

While history remains a constant in Venclova's poetry, it is only one dimension of his work. For if in 'Flight' Venclova has evoked the word 'fate', we understand, given the circumstances of the poet's life, this is not a term chosen lightly. Along with Venclova's engagement with the past, it is his stubborn belief that if individuals 'cannot choose their time or place', they can choose their actions within it. That it is each person's responsibility to reflect upon and understand the meaning of human agency, which is the source of personal ethics. In this, the reader of Venclova's work will also quickly suspect that the poet's choice of the title *The Grove of the Eumenides* for his work in Lithuanian and the present book is also far from arbitrary, pointing to yet another theme that runs throughout this volume.

The Grove of the Eumenides' titular poem unfolds in modern-day Greece, near Athens, among the ruins of the ancient site of Colonus at Agia Eleousa. The site, with its sanctuary for Theseus, was chosen by Sophocles as the setting for Oedipus's burial place in *Oedipus at Colonus*. In the poem's dialogue with Sophocles's play, Venclova evokes the spirits of the Eumenides, more commonly known in English as the Furies. For the poet is keenly aware – even if he is surrounded by a violence of modernity that deforms the ancient site – of the implications of individual action and reminds us of the force of these once feared deities:

A gesture from them can silence cypresses,
make planets cease to spin in distant heavens,
and sails hang limp on their black masts.

Such allusions in Venclova's poems, however, are far from mere classical or aesthetic tropes. Rather they bring us back to the importance of our choices, which are as inescapable as those of Oedipus and have far-reaching consequences:

We
grow blind and learn you can't deny your sin
as skies heat up and bodies turn to ice.

[tr. Rimas Užgiris]

With progressive readings we come to understand that at work in these late poems is both a personal and a generational reckoning. Like Oedipus, who returns to the grove of the Eumenides for his final days, Venclova in this volume looks back and takes an unflinching look at age, at personal and historical events, at the done and the left undone. In a similar way, in the poem 'The Way to Planty Park, Kraków', the poet surveys the epochs of his life, but even then, warns that there are still days ahead, cautioning us, evoking the Greek philosopher Solon, to 'Call no man happy until he's lived through all his appointed days.' Over the last decades, in contrast to much relativistic poetry in English, Venclova's work, with its immense lyrical beauty and philosophical stoicism, has been a welcome relief and ethical resource for many, as we face the results of our modern choices and their aftermath.

Such reflections are interwoven into the fabric of Venclova's poems with immense skill. For this reason, each subsequent reading continues to reveal additional archaeological layers. And, as with all great poetry that has 'mystery' in it – a quality prized above all by Akhmatova – the more we return to Venclova's poems, the more we find there. For in the sacred grove of the Eumenides there are further secrets for the ages, as the second part of Sophocles' play concerns itself with the folly of war and fratricidal strife.

And we also remember that it was at Colonus, in the sanctuary of Poseidon Hippios that – as chronicled by Thucydides and in line with Polybius's cycles – the fifth century BCE Athenian oligarchs plotted their coup and the reign of the Four Hundred came to pass. For the Athenians had failed to sufficiently cherish and protect their democracy, leaving it open to oligarchy. An event that, in these uncertain days, gives food for thought.

In this way, Venclova's long historical perspective does not imply a remove or lack of engagement with the times in which we are living, quite the contrary. The calamitous impact of the current war in Europe is also present in Venclova's new volume. His moving poem 'Azovstal', which addresses the tragic spring 2022 siege of the southern Ukrainian city of Mariupol, describes with bitter irony, and in unblemished terms, the brutality of war:

> Hail to you, forgotten Goddess of History!
> With your rocket-shell retinue, slaughtered soldiery
> We recognise you – emerging – that day of fear,
> When caterpillar treads and helicopters cross the border.
> [...]
> For Death is still young. She needs agility, time –
> To train, master her craft – slowly takes aim,
> Flails for a while: the body greeted by shrapnel
> Only after the fifth try – after, a dead lull falls. [...]
>
> [tr. Ellen Hinsey / Rimas Užgiris]

At the poem's end, Venclova evokes the bombing of the Azovstal steel plant where a final group of refugees and soldiers have taken shelter. He references the French general Pierre Cambronne who refused to surrender even if the battle was surely lost. But while in *The Grove of Eumenides* the classical, historical and the contemporary overlap, it is always the present and the living which most concern the poet, whose voice is frequently marked by poignant emotion – and a sadness for the world. In Venclova's poems we find a constant call for vigilance, while endurance and the drive for justice are understood as the foundational *sine qua non* of civil life in society.

Through Venclova's reminders of these ethical possibilities, a gift is restored to us: not a gift of pessimistic realism, but of a practical form of hope, that sustains our humanity and our capacity for compassion. We are called back to our responsibilities, our civic tasks – ever continuing. And in this, poetry and literature play a central role. For it is, above all, Venclova's enduring belief in the power of witness and speech that dominate his life's work. As with his previous books, in the present volume it is language that fortifies the spirit in dark times. We hear Venclova's determination and courage in a poem such as 'Before the Fort', which, while acknowledging the passage of time and the limitations of the alphabet, nevertheless affirms the latter's necessary and restorative power:

Whatever else, speak. Verse hardly holds what is pressed
Over time into the hardening clay of consciousness.
[...]

The keyboard flickers, a presence hovers that you but feel.
The mirror fades. Age enfetters the fatigued body alive.
You can't begin from the start, no matter how you strive.
Whatever else, now speak. There is nothing more real.

[tr. Rimas Užgiris]

For many over the decades, Venclova has been not only a critical poetic voice, but an intellectual and ethical resource, profoundly knowledgeable not only about the depths of the totalitarian experience, but also the spirit's capacity for renewal. In these days of the brutal return of History, his poems are more necessary than ever.

* * * *

The completion of this book was only possible through dialogue and collaboration with Tomas Venclova and partnership among its three translators. I am once again joined in this volume by Diana Senechal, the award-winning translator of Tomas Venclova's first volume in English, *Winter Dialogue*, as well as Rimas Uzgiris who has also become one of Venclova's foremost translators. Senechal, a poet, translator and educational theorist, is the author of the recent volume *Solo Concert* (2024) as well as two works of non-fiction. She generously contributed her time, despite her teaching responsibilities in Hungary, where she relocated in 2017. Of Lithuanian heritage, but raised in the USA, Rimas Užgiris is a poet, translator, editor and critic. After completing his PhD in philosophy at the University of Wisconsin-Madison, he relocated from the United States to Vilnius and is now an assistant professor at Vilnius University. Užgiris has edited and translated numerous books from Lithuanian, including a previous volume with Bloodaxe Books, *Then What* by Gintaras Grajauskas (2018). Full biographical notes on the translators are available at the end of this volume.

For their support during the preparation of this book I would personally like to thank Mark Carlson and Katharina Narbutovic for their help – both concrete and intangible. I am also grateful to Gerard Smyth at *The Irish Times*. Rimas Užgiris extends his warm thanks to Marius Burokas. Rimas Užgiris, Diana Senechal and I would also like to express our gratitude to the many publications where these translations first appeared. Finally, we above all extend our collective thanks to Tomas Venclova whose work, like Diogenes' lamp, continues to shine in the darkness of human history – past and present.

ELLEN HINSEY
Paris, 2024

I

On Both Sides of Alnas Lake

Where the young Czesław Miłosz used to swim

Open the shutter. The still dark stretch
is cut by a dock. The whispers of rushes carry
up from the lakeshore sparsely meshed
with wisps of juniper. A limpid dictionary!
The water secretes its smoke, rocking a boat,

a rough drop of air touches the throat,
burns the mouth's arch in a sudden blaze.
You can spot the footprints of a boar
by the gate. A swimmer in the waves
tests, as every morning, in a private war,

his strength against the contents of the lake.
The eyes can't take in the sleek plateau.
The head dives down. The spume of a wake
glints under a hand. Swallow speech echoes
and a cloud hollows into a sail-like shape.

The current stiffens, and the body revives.
The shore is near, the water like ice.
Praise the high creation of God – alive
with warbling and light whose rays race
to dandelion, water lily: their heads rise.

You touch a pine like a rosy column
and know – the world is wide and one.
Far away – thresholds, others' stairs, a foreign
forest, that bitter bread, an unexpected garden
by the Potomac or next to Montgeron.

The wind and the lungs are in league.
The common bleak breaks out from the depths,
and stings of premonition do not arrest breath –
the shadow which you will be recedes,
having beaten death with a paper's leaf.

The dew has dried, the young cheek burns.
Forms undergo alteration and saturate being.
Sharpening sight, ripening hearing:
stop for a minute with this blessing.
Above the cliff, autumn sounds its horns.

[RU]

To Master Radovan

On the coastal stretch between Aspalathos and Polai
(or Split and Pula), where Greek effortlessly
entwines the local dialect, and the walnut falls
on the smooth roadway, we sense each other's presence – briefly.
Clouds augur heat, shadows at intervals darken window
lattices and arches. On the square's left side is the portal,
ponderous as a litany. *Kyrie eleison*. The marble transcription
is meant for everyone – but best deciphered by God.
Two lions guarding the door are akin to those that once ministered
to Mark and Jerome. Behind them you can't yet envision
pilasters, vaults, or the tripart nave.
Seven hemispheres give form to a delusory universe –
whose final endpoints are Adam and Eve. The massive
bodies curve spacetime. Both already know shame –
but not yet death (this, the Lord will bestow).
Everything that happened next is a consequence of their fortuitous guilt.
Vine tenders, wild boar, deer, pursuits among the undergrowth
(in this stone thicket, you can hardly distinguish the hunter from hunted).
In December: suckling pigs are slaughtered; sausages are smoked in January.
An old man by a hearth – his gaze fixed on a pot,
a young man shearing sheep, his face ruddy from wind,
another – or perhaps the same – tilts an amphora
a third – or perhaps the same – is fitted with Roman armour –
because there will be soldiers always, like the eternal month of March and Mars.
All are self-portraits. You didn't want to finish elaborating
the cycle of the year – but the months rolled over the city's rooftops
and the Trecento stealthily approached, along
with the inexorable – such as wars, fevers, childbirth's pain,
and terminal disease. And Virgo, as now and forever –
revealed the Child to us or, rather – to the ineffable father.

I am no longer familiar with your prayers. Time erodes a stone's facing;
destroys the faces of the living. Only a name risks enduring –
but can also be bestowed upon those unworthy of it –
the sons of hatred. Evening. A speedboat flips through
the sparkling book of the bay. A sail and its reflection
imprint onto the water's surface like an Aleph.
A dove hovers over the tower. Radovan, perhaps someone
would say, it is your soul. But we were excluded from such a realm
the day we were cast out of paradise. Perhaps we are becoming water
reflections, gusts of wind, portal reliefs. This we must accept –
for this is our epoch.

[EH]

Dictator

In the factory, behind bars, or on the throne
he remained a peasant. He knew how to separate wheat
from chaff, to yoke muscular oxen. Thus, the farmer's expert
art was felt by tool and animal alike – including humans.
A whip. Straw. He knew from friends or enemies what to expect.
Then, having overcome all evil, he sought to fashion

a new being. Among city pleasures, he preferred the theatre.
For when the future neared, and almost all had wisely
confessed their errors, all he required was a stage.
Where once was wasteland, a Babylon of marble and jasper
arose. The colossal hall could enfold: St Peters,
Notre-Dame and Westminster – all at once – the enormous

balcony empty: so the silhouette on the terrace
became an exclamation mark to stun the masses – both spy and milkmaid –
on that vast expanse of Champs Elysées – laid
out after the original, but greater, and, alas, not in Paris).
Still, we frequently err. He entered a different Elysium field,
under charred earth, in the heat, beneath the tilted cross

and Red Star (asking both to have mercy upon him).
Above the grave, the fading national flag's colours,
and, like heads with open mouths, artificial flowers
puzzled, fill the faience of a stained cup's rim.
A leaflet flutters, embossed with: 'Thanks for freedom',
for to merely say *sic transit* would be too mundane.

Further off: deserted spaces, windows' worn playing-cards.
A strip of sky gleams like glue on an envelope
torn by a censor. The capital never learned to weep.
Rusty, sclerotic pipes. Joblessness and hardship.
A million homeless children (for he had abortion banned)
and stray dogs. Here, that Christmas never ends –

when a tarpaulin, like a bloodied husk was placed over,
and a dozen handfuls of black dirt covered
the one who believed, until death, he was loved by the people.
A crow reigns among leaves; meagre poplars rustle,
and a schoolboy closes a book, barely a second look,
never memorising his name.

[EH]

The Process of Beatification

Our knowledge of her life's end is limited.
Many witnesses perished, others – perhaps the most important,
died shortly after the war. Further: secrecy reigned.
Yes: the *Vel d'Hiver*. Refashioned waste bins
brought to safety four children (though
two hundred of them remained). In the shelter
she established years before, bed and sustenance
awaited escaped prisoners of war. A small printing press
fashioned identity papers, affirming the bearer
belonged to the proper race. Incidentally, guards
did permit – if but occasionally – comfort for
those condemned to death (a traditional rite,
never revoked in that quartier, since the Gauleiter
came from a Catholic family). Some sources state
she once spoke with a young girl in a cell,
who angrily proclaimed: 'This is rubbish –
there is no God. Because if there were,
He would release me from this prison.' The nun
knew only too well that God lay in
a bomb crater's abyss; in a pit,
a bullet through the back of the skull,
rotting beneath the tundra's lichen.
She therefore removed her nun's habit. Instructed the prisoner
to conceal her hair, skirt and shoes.
Then she sat on the bed; turned her face from the door.
The guard, arriving a moment later,
accompanied the timid black-cloaked silhouette
to the gate. No documents were checked.

We located the rescued woman a bit too late.
Her long life: spent by a railway's embankment.
Beyond her window, freight cars clattered by –
smoke pervaded the lungs' bronchi. Rainy mornings she ran late.
Rushed to work over footpaths strewn
with dirty leaves. One hour into the city,
to an office – that at the outset, offered income,
but like so many, went under with the world's
downturn. At the end of every month
the bills were daunting. The family was divided –
but then, it was hardly a family. An adopted daughter soon departed,
failed to write. Yolks hissed in the frying pan. Each night
the mirror showed: spreading wrinkles, flaccid breasts, protruding
violet veins. Solitude, the body's slow decline.
By the way, alcohol did its job as well.
As before, she mechanically made up her lips.
At night, in dreams, she sometimes saw the prison. During the day,
she tried not to recall it, then ceased to remember the whole affair –
due to Alzheimer's (to tell the truth, a sort of salvation).
No doubt, someone might ask: was the price too high –
to exchange fates with one of thousands, like a penny,
or postage stamp embossed with an illegible face?

We do not know how the nun perished. Perhaps
the gas chamber; perhaps injection by phenol.
Her own sins aren't hard to enumerate. A youth spent like Mary
Magdalene. Her own children unable to find their way.
Some occasional verse. Frequently bored at Mass –
she was known to chain-smoke Gitanes,
unbefitting of her nun's habit. But one thing is certain:
she never asked herself if it was worth the price.
As the Lord, whose place she fleetingly took, never asks.

[EH]

Before the Fort

Whatever else, speak. Verse hardly holds what is pressed
Over time into the hardening clay of consciousness.
There, we find contrasts of colours and fine detail,
The ocean's gleam, shame, wonder, and our travail.
Maybe after death. But the plane rolls down the runway.
Maybe when you won't exist. But a sentence has no fate.
Over the horizon's line, by the switchback – a medley
Of roofs. The citadel casts its shadow by Gurdić Gate.

Greet the scorched grasses, whose dry clumps lock up
The stretch of bay where nameless towns of stone
Age and decay. Thunderstorms slip along the strand
On the other side of the well-burnished slope.
Clouds. An untamed motorboat stirs the current alone
And from bay bottom raises Mediterranean sand.
Now, in the darkening mirror, you don't meet you.
A lamp, a keyboard, a dictionary. That much came true.

On the windward side of storms, at Europe's deaf edge,
Where you've been taken by fate or divine caprice,
You will lodge in darkness, as others have found a place
Beyond horizon's brushstroke or the switchback's ledge.
The keyboard flickers, a presence hovers that you but feel.
The mirror fades. Age enfetters the fatigued body alive.
You can't begin from the start, no matter how you strive.
Whatever else, now speak. There is nothing more real.

[RU]

Azovstal

Hail to you, forgotten Goddess of History!
With your rocket-shell retinue, slaughtered soldiery,
We recognise you – emerging – that day of fear,
When caterpillar treads and helicopters cross the border.

Then we grow accustomed to your rule. At first:
A high-rise's ruptured chest, trees ablaze on the coast,
Blasted train junctions, the endless steppes' theatre
Where, mired in black earth, Mazepa was cursed by Peter.

For Death is still young. She needs agility, time –
To train, master her craft – slowly takes aim,
Flails for a while: the body greeted by shrapnel
Only after the fifth try – after, a dead lull falls.

A drone traces an invisible path in the air.
The twenty-year-old guard slowly leads an elder
Behind a fence's shelter – what matter he's a civilian –
For both, the last few metres will only lengthen.

A pea coat's owner abandons one site of ruin –
Occupies another. A satellite docked in the heavens
Impassively looks on. Cannon blast a nitrogen cistern:
Ten blocks have been taken – *gloria nostra aeterna*.

How distant the harbours and train stations of salvation!
Facing the checkpoint: friend or foe? It's unknown –
Will they shoot or let you go – chickens left by gates
For looters, goats loose in yards – turn the gaze

To the map with unmarked *Trostyanka, Merefa, Irpin* –
With their torn-off roofs thrusting up through nettles,
And caught in the throat: the stench of those no longer,
While children learn to say 'traitor', 'rifle', 'hunger'.

A bullet, not a seagull, incises the low tide's line,
Beyond a broken window, a mirror reflects clear skies –
Descendants born in shelters will observe it with fear,
For not God's kingdom, but a sky of nuclear threat is near.

Clotted blood stains. The bass and alto of explosions.
For every Thermopylae there will be an Ephialtes.
Bid them farewell – for honour or shame, you don't know:
The path's cut off: in the end, the Medes will break through.

So then, Goddess of History, war remains war.
In a hostile city: a sunshine-struck boulevard.
A student under a linden grinds a cigarette into sand,
Repeats the old line: 'How sweet it is to hate one's fatherland'.

And the soldier – his comrades won't recall his patronym –
Subsists on stale air in the underground labyrinth,
Yet when his words cease, stone and concrete will repeat
The defiant riposte Cambronne hurled at his attackers.

[EH / RU]

Flight

A pilgrim, before boarding, kneels and prays in the presumed direction of the Kaaba.

Half-way through the ritual, I am guided by the covered passage to the cabin's illuminated space, where perhaps a breath of Europe's air still lingers.

There, a different litany awaits, witnessed a hundred times: instructions if the plane must land on water – or if the pressure drops.

Always the same slight discomfort when the wheels part from the runway and the terminal recedes in the distance, reduced to a pencil case.

Yet, what is death after so many years, landscapes, encounters – when your time is over?

Strata of clouds hang over the skyscraper-crowded bay, a weighty vault like Uranus consummating his love.

His union with Gaia begat Cronus: the one who devoured his own offspring.

In her womb, other deities were conceived: Oceanus and Mnemosyne.

Under the plane's wings, the familiar land spreads out – which shelters the wayfarer but is not destined to become native earth.

Rather, white wooden estates set in the shade of gardens between freeways: a small-sized town you'll never call home.

Then estuaries, archipelagos, Greenland's melting ice.

An almond-eyed stewardess pours wine for all who desire it.

Your coordinates are between Cap Farewell and the Hebrides, or perhaps between your era's polar points – its end and its beginning.

Continents, oceans and epochs overlap – one upon the other.

In the realm of Oceanus's sister Mnemosyne – as if on a seat-back screen – you observe the far north's tundras and ridges, the desolate steppes, the vast deltas of cold rivers – an *oikumene* destined for that time's generations.

Then slowly, you reinvestigate old spectacles: chains of trenches, artillery shells searing overhead, the words *Jedem das Seine*, and the unbreachable concrete walls behind which one couldn't make out prisons, streets, States.

Human beings cannot choose time or place. But they can choose their fate.

During these years you have said everything – or nearly – whispered to you by the *daimonion*.

You spoke darkly, obscurely, but as one of your interlocutors discerned, everything must be transmitted thus: lest one succumb to pride.

For everything incontestable or absolute issues from a world about which we know nothing, except that we would perish without it.

Scotland, Bergen. Well, my era has passed.

Some friends remain, their number diminished. Beauties who once took your breath away have already crossed the threshold of senility.

In another sequence of time, floorboards are warmed by sun – and pots of jam sit on veranda shelves.

Painted frescoes across a veranda wall, women in summer frocks pick apples and gather them up in baskets.

Set in a daguerreotype's oval: your grandmother after marriage. You haven't yet learned how she'll die. It's best not to know it.

Beds of nasturtiums, then a silver fir and orchard, where you bestowed the names of beasts from the fifth volume of zoologist Brehm – upon the trees.

And if these trees still remain, it is perhaps only in Plato's world or in the Lord's mind.

Then, from all around: the incomprehensible voices of your contemporaries. Tiny Towers of Babel upright in travellers' sweaty palms – marvels to which you'll also never become accustomed.

You only understand the fact that empires creak and nations deny each other's existence – and artillery, once again, finds plenty of employment.

Insurgents sleep in caves of clay and cars head out to dark suburbs. Multitudinous crowds flow through capitals' streets, many unaware of their own misery.

Corpses of fugitives adrift in Mediterranean boats and walls shelter the remains of old residents. *Jedem das Seine.*

The vault like Uranus consummating his love. And Cronus maturing in Gaia's womb.

[EH]

The Grove of the Eumenides

Now touch the wrinkled mallow's bud,
then climb the hill, look back, up north.
Cafés have closed, and wheels don't roll
along the city streets. Some homeless dogs
still snore where acacias shade syringes. Years
have passed since your last visit. Grapes,
bay leaves, and mostly mugwort. Pour
some honey for the mute sisters on the hill.

The weight of June makes cracks in clay.
You use the pupils of others' eyes to see
the humid air that quivers above the sea,
where scattered rays like Doric columns cleave
the sky and cradle a crumbling day.
A fortress hides among the roofs in mist.
Now meet your fate not in Athena's place,
nor Thebes', but in what is left of Colonus.

The crowded suburb rests, silent under sun.
The gods have changed, Ananke aged.
A ditch of thistles holds a piece of peristyle,
which may be more Idea now than porch.
A runner panted here then met his fate.
The Lord Almighty plays with us while we
grow blind and learn you can't deny your sin
as skies heat up and bodies turn to ice.

The patient Eumenidean spring has dried.
What once were Erinyes now scorn all discord.
A gesture from them can silence cypresses,
make planets cease to spin in distant heavens,
and sails hang limp on their black masts.
The osprey now is all that moves:
it scours the sea in vain for prey,
its fall like that of Icarus ignored.

You are behind the times already. It's late.
The wise men said it's best to not be born,
and if you were, then not for long. Cement
now covers sacred slopes. Instead of Theseus,
an ant is left to lead, and inch by inch
it navigates the ruin, wrecking rhythm on its way.
Will lightning strike, or storm wipe us away,
or will the earth split open? The Judge should know –

But what if He does not? This place now sleeps
and sinks into a smog as into steamy sheets –
into the bitter scent of mint, or drought,
or nothing. Olive leaves blush and burn.
An ancient alphabet grows black here, etched
on windowpanes where roofs ascend the slope.
The quickly broken echo of a sigh
now deepens in summer's heavy silence.

[RU]

II

South of the Prospect

Secondary, mostly tranquil – but periodically renamed
In various languages, the *locus amoenus* of our youth
Ran between the brewery, wet archways, scarred plaster
And a statue: threatened each decade with demolition.
The path to school, as before the war, in a bygone State.
February's sun lingering on brick walls – still the same.

An indifferent capital, a poor city of the provinces.
We were only a few – most came from other places.
But all immediately understood: the Empire could
Break you. If midnight visitors knocked, next came
The unknown (in truth, known to everyone). But
Our time was a bit different: closer to a quagmire.

Our former rooms are astonished at our presence.
Hills by decaying walls no longer recall the words
We exchanged back then, glancing over shoulders,
Not unlike older generations conspiring in penury,
Striving to change the world. Thank God we didn't
Crave power. If anything: just to be remembered.

All now transformed into faded paper, to silent air.
In a wheelchair, one does not recognise a friend.
The stout old woman (a former beauty) collapses
Bedside, before work. The stylish man is defeated:
By drink, lung cancer. Not history, but commonplaces
Drive them into darkness. Even if history tried its best.

Late, between hills and gables of a vanished century,
I catch only white noise from the no man's land,
Where their wit, prayers, and quarrels have faded.
If I try to reach them, they mostly fail to answer –
Just pause in twilight. If they respond, it's hard to
Discern if it is them, or the One, who always *is*.

[EH]

Chinese Impressions

I *Probably En Route to Chengdu*

The alarm clock from the market in Hong Kong
stammers before seven. Its sharp-tipped stinger
writes 'To the station' in my mind.
For two weeks now, the country beyond the windows
is one in which I feel I haven't even been.
Rectangles compete to cover the curves of roofs
with images of the Leader and '...boro'.
(Who will win, no one knows.) Bicycles
lacquered in mud ride over splinters of bamboo.
Foil, tin, and cardboard lie in the avenue's hands.
A soulless landscape from dreams yet to come –
when loam and sand will press on your face
and your lungs will no longer draw air.

A crowd that could challenge Genghis Khan,
but the silence is deafening on the train.
Skyscrapers and a dilapidated temple
will soon be replaced by the fog of fields,
red sorghum, and weeping willows wading
into canals – the life that resists
every dynasty. The heart misses a beat.
When heaven turns away from a country,
there remains only commerce: petty gifts
for errant masses. The Wall is shabby,
the train car is over-full, and divinity
has vanished (if it ever was). That's partly why
one has to choose necessity –
to have the same worries, a different death –

and call it fate, but that's not right.
Another word would be better, not 'fate',
but there is no ideogram for that. Wisdom
is rarely born out of pain – more often of
surrender, hypocrisy, and bitter subterfuge.
You are this morning an illiterate
barbarian. It's doubtful you will return
to this land you lose with every instant,
and it, losing you, does not listen
to your speech. The Other surrounds you.
Here is soil that has soaked up a thousand years
of bones and fear. Here is the universe in which
you understand that eternity, withholding happiness,
will not free you from pity and the human chain.

II *The Mandate of Heaven*

The empire is ruled today by a clarified September
that strews the park with fragments of burnished altars.
The temple's three-storey dome gives relief from the heat
as if we were the gods. We seem to stand on the universe's shore.
Cicadas and birds are silent. No silhouette looms on the ochre
horizon whose patience is virtue – not a cloud graces the sky.
Extinguishing his cigarette, my friend continues: 'But I
think, of all the writings from up north, we can best relate

to *The Captain's Daughter* (here it's been renamed
The Miracle of Reciprocal Love). Our languages are estranged,
our military ranks differ, but the essential story is the same:
a robber struggles through a blizzard, an axe under his coat,
born from dirt and hunger. The threat grows less remote,
until nothing turns into everything. Nomadic gangs approach
the capital. Gongs ring out in alarm. In the unfettered chaos,
only the young versifier will escape the fateful noose.

'We have been reading it for two centuries, his story ended
well: the youth is saved by a girl, the rebel quartered,
but the wisest understand that sometimes it turns out worse:
the Guard surrenders its weapons, the bonfires are not lit,
the ruler runs barefoot across the plains (with arrows
fast on his heels), the minister's head rolls into a ditch,
and the palace servants and eunuchs (left alive, of course)
teach dynastic gestures to the victorious peasant hero.

'He strews rice, he bows, respecting his forefathers' ways
so that the kind heavens might increase the poor yield,
but secretly dreads poison in porcelain cups, erroneous
ideograms, spells, prefers not to speak at length in fear
of the wise men of his court, trusts only the steel of his blade,
feasts without pleasure because he knows he will throw it up,
and at night, blowing out the lantern, he prays to his divinities,
whose signs are not complex: a stake and bloody spear.

'His sons, one by one, live out their lives in senselessness.
The sixth, tired of killing, squeezes the state in his fist.
His concern is the rhythmic turn of the world's axis,
and he cleans the nomads off the steppes, stops the floods.
Provinces increase their tribute. North and South are wed
as male and female. Each year sees enough harvest
to keep the army up. The Lord laughs with his youngest wife,
and the bedstead is adorned with the sign for success in life.

'The grandson is different: he practises witchcraft, tries
to learn new chapters of the *Tao Te Ching* until dawn,
and takes counsel from geomancers, considering plans
to perfect the calendar and properly mark his haunts
in order to push back the instant when he will turn to ashes
and dust, just like some commoner. But their magic is a lie.
Of him, the fragmentary pages of chronicles mention two phrases:
'The constellations go out when I die,' and, 'I Want.'

'We can skip the next generation until we reach the final scion
of the tribe. His mouth has a bitter taste, his chest only pain.
There will be no posterity because there is no lover,
not even a man, to ignite the fire of an impotent emperor.
The capital degenerates. Foxes and demons breed in park grass,
acacias crack shingles. The empire sinks in the haughtiness
of a baneful, bright September. One can only guess in which province
Pugachev – as you call him – sharpens his battle axe.

'Even though dates and places change, we probably won't escape
the Wheel. But the poet of the North – or ours – still sees, I think,
something higher than fate. To speak in a noble strain – it's a string
his fingers pluck, the only thing that can push away the clanging
chains of echoing time. Yellow earth is carried away by the wave
that washes away the gallows, palaces, rebels, love, and graves,
and though the wisest one knows this process will never end,
a brush or plume remains for his hopelessly hurrying hand.'

III *Tea House in a Settlement: Variation*

On a wooden bench, among the irises of a garden bed,
where the shade of branches trips over a teacup's hue,
I exchange remarks about the weather with the dead,
and watch, as they do, the swollen, polluted blue –

it is as it was, though more refuse has come to line
the shore, and barges are now more common than junks.
Each person finds his or her habitual place in time,
grows bored, curses fate, and plays mahjong.

The shades exchange platitudes: 'Today is cooler', 'Move aside',
'The packet-boat is late' or, 'Am I where I should have been?'
I am also a shadow to them. It's not clear (what is there to hide?)
which of us is the negative and which the positive film,

what is reality and what a reflection, what is *perfectum*
and what the passing *praesens*. Here Asia sinks into the sea.
Like spiritualists, holding hands on a creaky table, we
foreigners begin to doubt again: maybe this is just a dream –

the canal, the ferns, the jujube, the word, 'really',
and the word, 'probably', and the Teahouse where
we find each other as the centuries dissipate in air
like steam, and a sleepless flame melds soul to body.

IV *In the Institute's Park*

There are only two such statues left in the city. They loom
between arborvitaes, one opposite the other. The buttons
of the tunics, the buns of the cheeks, are like peas in a pod.
The state is strong when discipline makes chaos uniform –
the students know this

who hammer away at intricate integrals and classics
here in the shade. The plaster crumbles – is sometimes patched.
The statues could be wisdom teeth in a black mouth ringed
by asphalt lips. Rain, seeping through cracks, corrodes:
monuments can't avoid cavities

nor the rot of roots. But it's pleasant in their shade
to turn the eyes away from the page and meditate
on this and that: the server's skirt in the cafeteria,
last night's draught of liquor, a dusky hutong, or even
about everything that extends

on this side of the Wall. Timeless vignettes: the old man bent
under bags of manure; the ox in the flooded field; jade dew
on lotus leaves; women whispering by a doorway
about how it's not worth it for their children to remain
under these skies of clay –

better to move away (taxes, the district chief, the failed harvest).
Nomadic camps in train stations which servants of order can't erase –
they themselves probably come from the next village over.
The teacher of calligraphy dreams in his narrow flat how once
his students beat him –

most tried to flog him without pain, but they followed orders
to the letter. Piles of dusty cement stretch out farther
than the eye can see, and beyond the strait: glass towers
rise like crickets, dragonflies, grasshoppers,
pretending, for that matter,

to be dead (who knows whether the shoe will fall).
Or another landscape: the tawny silvered air
of high peaks, a punctured skull in the bushes.
He to whom it belonged is not in Buddhist paradise:
he is not and never was at all.

Prayer flags and rosaries, losing their powers, become
products, like little yak-bone boxes; a person can live
without freedom, but not without barley porridge,
a bit of sleep, a coin. It's only hard to die without it:
but they died just the same.

The monuments age and crack. The portrait grows fatigued,
though refreshed each year, and stares hard at the deaf
and speechless square – the country's centre of gravitation.
The geometry of the abyss. Purling water washes away
scraps of music, silence,

and what remains of blood. One hundred or so metres away
stood a man, unarmed, who tamed an approaching tank
for an instant. He exists somewhere, uncaught, unknowing
that his incomprehensible gesture took the world's breath away.
In truth, it doesn't concern him.

v *High Plateau*

Yak wool wears down gravel.
A knife unseals blue meat.
The wildered wasteland kneels
where dawn fails to make heat.

Empty vaults ripple over monk
cells that have lost all sense of a plan.
The nirvana of the cloister's skeleton
is exchanged for rock and sand.

Clouds crack and crumble like frescoes,
even the cliffs seem to break and bend,
as if it all happened so long ago,
as if the war had now come to an end.

[RU]

Landscape with Polyphemus

In ruddy mountain depths – deep caves drone in emptiness.
Cold frosts the path. Water trembles in clear autumn's reign.
Like an attentive blind man, the landscape snares our voices –
With its calloused ears, its knots of nerves, its giant's brain.

Don't hide from fate, relish the day and, thick with salt,
The line of spume that marks the sand at low tide.
Wind plucks at trees and ruffles grass, empties the fireside –
Its pit blackens far away, on the heights, like an eye-socket.

The sky purifies, and God's hands crumple the star-map.
Bright lights all night: November flashes white copper.
The Leonids pound city thresholds with interstellar flak,
While channels and cliffs darken to death in a twofold fire.

[RU]

Three Imperfect Sonnets

I *Piazza Mattei*

A stained white cornice. Clouds. '...*Caesius fecit.*'
Clusters of grapes frame a cohort of brazen words.
Bells, like the pulse in the tyrant's aorta, grow quiet,
their faint peals fly across Largo di Torre. Here, no sword
can cleave reality from image. Ephebes gesture in the dusk,
and crystal rolls from a turtle's shield into a dolphin's
jaws, splashing a phallus. Acanthus and jasmine
become columnar stone like Daphne hiding from Phoebus.

Piazza Paganica, Via dei Funari.
The key rattles the door, unlocking Rome –
the gristle of the Palatine, the soil of the rotting Forum,
a lost century, with February forgotten already.
Only the fragments of letters fasten yesterday to today.
The fountain murmurs. Damp March drifts away.

II *Caffè Greco*

The points of needles prick the rosin-filled air.
Pine canopies sway. Sandstone heats and wears.
This city prefers repetition. Perhaps the terrorist
who finished off Moro is more timorous than Brutus,
perhaps the water more turbid (but as bland and capricious),
but he is not as old as the angular torsos of Caesars.
The alley, as before, branches from the Corso;
cumuli crowd its vantage, resembling ruins and frescos.

A café. An oasis choked with nomadic clamour.
In the depths of pale etchings – a doubled Rome,
baroque shells, spirals and the aquamarine Tiber.
An echo in the terrace lasts longer than a poem,
and the sun, unseen by those who have passed withal,
paints the fruit and erases shadows from the wall.

III *Colle Aventino*

'It didn't help either that he rejected the crown.'
Burdock rubs against the fur of a cat gone feral.
Motorcycles startle the block which once looked down
without fear on the prostrate body of the triumvir –
but enough of that. A siren sharper than a dagger
pierces the crossroad. Its drone drifts farther
into the hills above the Circus Maximus, then
to cool carnival booths in the square of Aventine,

packed with wine and cherries. Beyond gardens,
like a second sky, a cupola rises, speaking *urbi*
et orbi. Pink suburban stucco and the chapped skin
of roof shingles slowly soak up doubled Imperial
time. The universe brightens. Midday grows chilly,
and an ephemeral gaze embraces the eternal city.

[RU]

'The stream of smoke dissolved in yesterday's air'

The stream of smoke dissolved in yesterday's air,
While raindrops steamed in the passing day, marred
With mud. The sky now sighs, and earth's exterior
Stiffens within the links of time and longitude's bars.

The harmony of water and wind, enriched with ash,
Whose heavy greyness saturates the wings of birds –
Our veins and bones come undone in a sudden flash
Of flame, while ash and space disseminate our words.

Along stretches of sand, a beetle marks its path
With feelers. A stranger's footprints fade in gravel
And the eye avoids shadows in piney depths –
Knowing the soul will become a star, or a fossil:

The kind that will never be dug up from its rest,
But will abide in darkness, a diamond turning back to coal,
Or rather, like an ammonite shard, compressed
In Silurian layers: a bristly piece of the cosmic whole.

[RU]

Prehistory

I

To recognise the unwelcoming places where you grew
up in another land, before the last century was through:
a fruitless stretch of dunes, willows, a warehouse wall
by the shore will hardly recall who lived here at all.
The lonely rushed through these streets with a taxi and three
carriages, while orangeade dripped on park paths. At three-thirty,
German girls gathered on the other side of the tracks,
saying *Süsses Kind* over the strollers along their path.
They yearned for the empire's signs, walked the yellow
sand, and applauded the shadow on the balcony in the old
town, until their hairdos, hats, and rings were sunk
in bland waters by Marinescu in his victorious sub.

II

There is more to the landscape: importantly – the sky
and the piercing waves that gaze right into its eye,
smokestacks, stork-nest poles, willows sparsely
scattered along the lower banks of the canal,
the stink of flatfish, the wind rocking a shabby
yacht by the bridge. I see the teacher, holding his key,
returning from the Red Cross for a nap –
he gazes joylessly over his temporary flat:
laundry hung to dry in the garret, shutters knocking,
plaster peeling (onto the cradle?), bookshelves leaning
from Marxist tomes, and beyond the Danė river, he sees,
like a monotonous echo, timber frame homes recede.

III

The clatter of hooves – spoons and faience ring in answer.
The eye can spot a low Anglican church by the harbour.
Its roof is like the cover of an earthenware jar.
Nothing further. Europe's threshold or boundary –
these flat shores, these swamps, fertilised equally
by the bones of Skalvians, Old Prussians, Vistula Veneti.
Catalogues of the past: *nach Osten, Westen*, one flees –
ships are sunk, the implacable weight of the sea
presses mustard gas drums. An irresistible current:
its echo bursts repeatedly on the desolate grassy fort.
And so the limpid reflection below a frozen skiff gleams
in morning cold, clearer than the skiff itself, it seems –

IV

so deep, like a voice hardly recognised in a dream
but which, in repeating a pointless sound, can mean
more than the people to whom one speaks. A nymph,
unsleeping Echo, reigns over the world that is left.
Above the vanished city of my birth, from Bothnian
skerries to Skagerrak, from the fuming Eastern
Cape to Spit's End, a clear rhythm, as from a trumpet,
sails out beyond us, announcing the Last Judgement:
it will wake us in the dark, lead us home from imprisonment,
so that we might be thankful for everything – even when
time erases all shape and gesture, like an experienced
censor, from the sheet of paper, the photo, and the text.

[RU]

Cavalryman near Seinai

Beyond boulders and thaw, in a birch thicket,
A sharp-sighted foe watches the rider-poet
Who presses his spurs into a horse's flanks
and gallops off. Below the hill, a lake

Caked in ice stretches to greet him, his wrists
Wrapped in reins, the damp cold frosts
His spyglass. Now a mile from the front line
He catches up with his men in time.

A pot simmers in the clearing: the Uhlans
Knew there would be no attack till dawn.
Through hornbeams he watched the red sun
Wane. A bivouac awaited him on the rough lawn.

His heart, as always, was steady in its beat.
He wouldn't die: partings are not his fate,
Nor the machine-gun chattering at his feet,
Protected as he is by heaven's golden gate.

No, he is destined for decades of maturation
And endurance, to write deathless poems,
To live on in love's playful seductions,
In a happy capital, after a war well won.

[RU]

Beyond St Anne's and the Bernardines

I dream of hunchbacked Tiflis...

OSIP MANDELSTAM

Beyond St Anne's and the Bernardines,
where the liturgical calendar
is marked by a family of bells,
the monastery is held
within sand, hills, and all that is green.

Under high windows: ripples of rills
wander between steep gaps of hills
roof-tiles sketch harmonious lines,
and a street-light shines
double in pavement and sky.

On this side of three crosses,
the city fits into one's palm,
and a Doric column answers
cold frost with lucid calm:
I am full of weightless time.

The pavements are unhoned –
white planes laid out like books
scattered slant and oblique
where strings of streets break
and paint strips down to stone.

Not yet destroyed by wars,
unchanged by passing years,
the stone wall stretches under tin
guarding an unlocked labyrinth:
a realm of rough inscription.

In the market's dense disorder,
you drink a draught of wine –
and thanks to it, the unending whine
of your unfamiliar neighbour
becomes a speech more dear.

The linden leaf is fated to fall,
the grass to grow, the jay to fly,
death to wander down the street,
and you to recall the stanza's *why*,
relishing the richness of vowels in speech.

Twilight falls – a kind of innocence,
donning the mask of loneliness.

[RU]

Extra Urbem

Well, winter approaches and olive trees
begin to rustle under the cover of clouds.
(Here, an address is befitting: 'My friend
Septimius.') Seawater endures, unchanged
from the days when the Ligurian boats
conceded to Roman triremes. Only stiff
cliffs, supplanting our cities' barren
silhouette, erode: now slightly concave.

This stifling alphabet of rock and time.
Sandstone neumes, fermatas of marl.
Paths flooded by avalanche: darkened
tunnels vanish into a mountain's womb.
A gorge's waterfall feverishly argues
with itself, and a statue, which no one
will hew from its marble chrysalis,
eternally ages in a godforsaken mine.

We can barely distinguish direction –
the sky's vault opaque as the stone slope.
The hill's scar broken by a vertical.
A village emerges through wet fog,
resembling Rubik's variegated cubes,
scattered on the shore by the sea –
an island that has surrendered to trade,
the restive crowd, uproar, and filth.

The imperiousness of watery streets
brings a whisper from the Mezzogiorno.
We contend to have nothing in common
with armoured mussels, morays, slithery
sea predators, but most likely we err.
Plankton struggles in the seaport's grip.
After us, Septimius, this plankton will
prevail, much older than Liguria's boats.

We don't know to where things vanish,
but one thing is clear: *mare* will endure.
Here, where our women dry their hair
and wet umbrellas restively glisten,
and farinata graces the festive table,
centuries hence starfishes will encroach,
fish will glide by, mirrorlike or pyriform,
errant spray will dissolve. And the salty

current will fill this arrowed crevice –
for now still tunnelled, with tourists
in the churchyard, shops with shawls,
a plump baby in a pram, who glimpses
his or her earliest shapeless dream,
and the widow who each week waits
for waning guests, letters, phone calls,
and death (which frequently procrastinates).

Still, Septimius, we are free to choose:
fate is blind, but sound is clairvoyant –
music obeying not Ananke, but rather
two quarrelling sisters – two contrarian
queens: the first one Gaia who, from
her ancestor Chaos, inherited his grim
physique, his faceless force. The second:
the goddess of winds and solitude.

Let us be thankful to both sovereigns –
I prefer the one who dwells in air.
As the salty depths expand, and heat
menacingly presses on the surface of bays,
she performs her duty – she is friend
to cicada and thyme, she confers peace
upon the world's void. Let us listen
to her incessant, but reticent, voice.

[EH]

Caligula at the Gates

Our respite was short-lived in the end.
But after long hardships, it had seemed
It would never draw to a close. Friends
Invoked poetry and feasted in gardens,

Schools upheld the spirit of wisdom,
Flute-tones sailed under arcades' white,
Markets rustled in the squares each day,
And galleons transported holds of spice.

We marvelled at colour-washed mosaics
And were tempted by sun ripened fruit,
We ridiculed the words of the prophets –
But, agelessly, they proved to be true:

The room is besieged by clashing steel,
The heavens darken; the sea's forces rage.
Blow out the candles and close the gates.
Beyond them - Caligula and the plague.

[EH]

III

August Elegy

For Z.B.

How are you, how is it to live
in the zone unknown to us still?
Forgetful and wet to the full,
the seasons float over the gulf.

Heat presses the narrow pavement,
the helicopter hones its direction,
takes notice: someone is absent.
This barely was able to happen.

Caught in the battered ships' crush,
the whirlpools thrash the pavement,
and midyear soon comes to the seventh
year of your growing absence.

From that silent place what will I glean
on the balcony, pouring my wine
without you – who conquered alien
beds and bodies, you, sceptic, twin,

soul-likeness of mine? Almost always
you guessed what I had up my sleeve.
Now nature is all you have left –
the one God in whom you believed,

who always offered a safe
retreat from the State and its madness,
and whom – thrush's skill, lynx's craftiness –
you held higher than yourself.

Perhaps you are really in the fog,
in the film of glittering oil,
in scattered letters and logs,
by the promenade, where yachts jostle,

where road-loops are etched on the slope,
where the bell is contained in a breath
(a friend does not stay there long,
while an enemy stays to the death).

Perhaps you are really in the rays
where molluscs polish the deep,
in Vingis's rusty pines,
and in Kotor's salt molecules,

over here, where the sea vapour clears,
and in sands a thousand versts away.
'It is good,' you yourself would say,
'that nature gets by without tears.'

[DS]

Notes on Xenophon

Grass in the fire,
pebbles under the shoe. Will the mosque's bayonet
bow to the rocket? Shapes form in the air:
decrepit clay walls, homestead silhouettes.
Settlements, not worth the pain of restoration,
poppies and death mark out the contours of the region.

A precipice,
which heaven itself can't make out through the dust,
the trudge of ancient hoplites, horsemen, tanks
in the meridians between the Indus and the Euphrates.
A game without compassion, plan or rules
trades harvest cycles for meagre saline soils.

Next to the square,
a young man comes to a stop, adjusts his belt,
then brings both hands together near his heart,
gives thanks to the Lord, looks to the sky, and steps
into the void. Darkness. Several corpses
are captured on the smartphones of reporters.

Not letting up,
soaring this way and that over cracked terrain
through skirmish and gunshot, combing every slope,
the unmanned aircraft buzzes like a hornet.
The bearded target will not be killed today,
since his hiding place is next to the embassy.

In the lagoon, crossing
the water's rainbows, stiff mines drift
and a cutter sinks. In the maelstroms *apparent*
rari nantes, which the mainland will not miss.
The roughened wave is full of oil and grease,
the bottom is far, and the sea couldn't care less.

A sizzling day.
On the central street, trade is again booming,
the international zone forgets about the bombings,
the soldier is greeted by a brothel's dull display
by the cemetery fence, where earth has been upended,
and bones raised airward sooner than portended,

since TNT,
what shall we say, outdoes the trumpet's call,
and retribution is far harsher than guilt
(which a historian says is largely mythical).
Yet at these latitudes Jugurtha already could
figure out how to be both violent and shrewd.

At the heart of hush,
in the peaceful outskirts, someone glued
to a phone or flickering screen becomes inured
to a plain truth: all those with bodies die,
a corpse in the desert is detail, trifle, fuss,
and, like the horizon, purpose recedes from us.

And in rubble, again,
armies are stuck and nations cross each other,
the highways choke under the cloudy cover.
Later: the impasses. Later a vault remains,
like a kishlak panting rancour from the heart,
where the palm cracks and the zodiac falls apart.

[DS]

Death of the Argonaut

When he returned, the land was not the same.
Behind a crumbling rock, a river foamed,
Ancient like him. Thorns and shells stuck
To the bottom of his feet. The cypresses were gone.
In the valley where the Centaurs used to roam,
A shallow, sleepy city had been built,
Where no one had an inkling of his ship.
Since infancy, the dwellers knew one thing:
When pain and ruin visit this peaceful shore,
They always have one origin: the sea.

Under the low billows flashed the fish –
The only interlocutors remaining.
He started to forget it all himself.
Had mountains loomed over Colchis, was there
An armed regiment, sprouting from the ground,
But to be vanquished by a plough, harnessed
To two fire-nostrilled beasts? His consciousness
Had lost all traces of the wild-born princess
With her unruly curls and strange eyes.
(By now she would have gone completely grey.)

Stuffy heat, still several dozen steps.
A promontory. Matted lagoon algae.
Two islands, like a body cleaved in two.
She said: we die and are again reborn,

But she didn't want to recreate a thing.
At best, she gave a new birth to herself
At dawn when, after unrelenting struggle,
She lay abundant with his sweat and seed;
In silence, she just multiplied being
By makeshift yet eternal nonexistence.

The waves erase the traveller's footprints.
At the slope, a slum. Its ridges are surpassed
By the ribs of an immense ship in the sand.
His eyes did not expect that framework.
Here is a bed, different from former times.
He lies under the ship, far from the sun.
The day has passed, now it is time to rest.
How many tides have chopped against this keel!
A shade is thrown onto his temple by
Its wheel, once broken by the Symplegades.

[DS]

'Tell me, what did you love? One city you left behind'

Tell me, what did you love? One city you left behind,
Carnal mysteries, Haydn, the ochre of a misty pastel,
A lagoon slope filled with women's shouts, children at play,
A lamplit manuscript (or candle-lit, better still).

Those you never met will now start the game again.
The old coin loses its relief, the profile its weight,
What belongs to the cosmos will return to the silent cosmos;
To convert your soul into verse, you spent all your fate.

You won't foil the gods with mighty-armed Perseus's shield.
Your eyesight gives up and your hearing holds out in vain,
And a storm encrusts the breakwater's ridge with ice,
And, dismantling the heavens, darkness floats onto the plain.

[DS]

Mother of the Living

Alone they stayed together – man and wife,
the angel having banished them and vanished;
yet mountain peaks still harmonised on high,
the echo wandered in the gorge's bends,
and all things were a gift of God – the lines
in Adam's face, the robe with its coarse fabric,
and creekless, desiccated and forlorn,
a landscape overgrown with briar and thorn.

The stone did not yield readily to their hands.
Thirst tore her throat, the fields bore little grain.
Her fingers stiffened under the heavy spade,
her legs gave way, her waist bent under strain.
Adam, returning home at dusk, bewailed
the time spent hunting, gathering in vain,
and turning his attention to the tent,
taught the tamed beast the ways of settlement.

At night she gave up rest for pleasure's soul,
her body faithful to the lunar phases.
She waited. God was generous with her.
In pain she bore sons, as He had promised.
The younger one was eloquent and skilled,
but a hundred times dearer was the prodigal
first-born. They are not hard to tell apart,
for one of them brought death to Earth.

The tribe is growing. Death is not so hard.
My lips have trouble speaking those same words.
My cartilage is fragile, eyesight dark,
my long-lost dreams of Paradise gone dim.

Barely, just barely dropping from the clouds,
water moistens the soil. Shrubs surround;
and their stiff leaves are troubled by a blast
of desert wind ripping from the south-east.

To herdsmen – herds, to her – the household chores.
While night lasts, it shines above: a fragment
of a garden long closed to the likes of man,
a star no more expansive than an atom,
and the mother gazes at it all alone,
since by now God has taken away her Adam,
deprived of past and present, branch and foliage,
she has grown ancient, like the tree of knowledge.

Inside her womb, the universe matured.
Her veins gave life and form to Messalina
and Joan of Arc. She gave birth to a daughter
who gave her head to save a neighbour's life
in a KZ barrack. Another daughter buried
a newborn in the trash, without grief;
she left him there though his heart still beat,
a baby she conceived one drunken night.

And she bore the One to whom the whirlpools cede,
who pulls anchors from the lagoon's deep floor,
for whom the vault lights flame and flame away,
wrapping a secret shrine within their fire –
that future Mother whose resplendent glory
the portals of basilicas proclaim,
for they live on, and breathe throughout the ages –
baroque spheres, gothic ogival arches.

[DS]

'It's not instantly clear why it rises so rich'

It's not instantly clear why it rises so rich
In the vision, as if a strong lens had refined it;
An Art Deco ornament seen through a breach
In the branches, a staircase, a sprawl of old ivy.

Steps can be heard before noon on the street,
Their sound stops short of the garden terrace,
Caged by the air, the bluish dome sleeps,
And your sight reaches far – to Aleksotas.

(Yes, it's insomnia. With feeling blind fingers
You push back this pressure of contours and shapes,
Not sure until dawn if the Lord will allow you
To sink into dreams – more precisely, to wake.)

Where the two rivers join, summer leans long.
So white are the alleys, so easily bungled.
Your schoolfriends have scattered, each to his home.
Between sunny street blocks, childhood has lingered.

There, the serried acacia is severed by sabres
Of rays. August squints while shining the streets
(Which stubbornly kept their pre-Soviet names –
Gediminas, *Maironis*, *Kęstutis* and *Freedom*).

At the kiosk, a crowd. You drink lemonade.
Your palm wipes a drop of sweat from your brow,
The walk to the Old Town completed, your gaze
Barely glimpses two swans in the pharmacist's pane.

In the barren apartment, a young woman's voice
Intones your imminent, lonely fate –
The roadside stone will not understand
The tiny wanderer. Enough of your straining

To catch the humorous note that rolls
In her mouth just like the stone of her song.
Your mother is thirty-four years old.
Only ages later will you carry her urn

Now along different stones. Up a steep road,
Just the two of you, as in the room of the past.
'Are you tired? Let's wait. It is not far away.
Only fifty more metres. Then we will rest.'

[DS]

From the Future

In a minute the rain will lift.
Darkness deepens over the waters.
At the city gates, grimy sails, cutters
and skiffs manoeuvre the drift,
and the brine is surprisingly stiff.

You ascend to the precipice near
the rim of the bay at evening,
where seagulls visit the railings
and the spume on the concrete turns clear,
and the latch has been locked for a year.

The lock groans under the strain.
From the highway, a child's voice echoes,
and an ululant siren answers
the lamp that is forced to shine.
I didn't foresee you alone,

but alone you are. The dimmed port
is embraced by the blackening pool.
Well, instead of a cheek that is absent,
let coffee bring warmth to your hands.
Steam spreads, your head starts to spin.

Outside the house where you stay,
the death-swelling firmament murmurs.
I might hold back its blow for a moment.
While your palm holds the heavy key,
in the darkness remember me.

[DS]

Kotor Sun

Come to my lips, let me whisper what I have found:
the darkness of our death is no match for these –
the pebbled paths, the stone of this narrow fjord,
the stoic rule of the diamond Ionian seas.

The eyelids, the failing retina keep them figured
where a piercing beam let loose a hostile spray
when the day froze, and the eyeball was transfigured
to teach us to save time – or forgive it, anyway.

Beyond the horizon, flame and war rage on.
We won't come back. A tongue of foam will outlive us,
the grasses gripping the cliff, this foreign lagoon,
and grazing the bottom, the large and somnolent fish.

The dim walls descend from the bell-tower to the pier.
The roof tiles lap up the white of the cooling air.
Don't fear, I have the silver obol right here;
for the boat drawing near, this is surely enough for our fare.

[DS]

Eos

The stiff breaths of October drive the boat forth.
She will soon make her way around the pulsating lighthouse.
    The sea opens up to her
        From cloudy Istria

To the cliffs of Leucada. A fisherman, exhausted
By the cold, drags the bay's slippery bounty.
    Greek bread and wine
        Sleep in his flesh and veins.

So death recedes. Morning approaches with a rooster's cry
And a swallow takes heed – there, beyond the watershed,
    Where Aegeus, misled
        By a taut black sail

Drank of the wave. Tonight you are alone.
You rely on the motor, finding in the seaside sand,
    Decades later, a trace
        You left of yourself.

A bed of heather, a stone instead of a pillow.
A woman's voice in the yard, dispelling deep sleep.
    While you were absent,
        Time passed in a different way.

The foam wets the sails and burns the whites of your eyes.
A stubborn ray of sun hits your temple aslant
    To freeze into your iris
        The geometry of the clouds.

[DS]

IV

Hamden, Connecticut

The water washed over the weir's concrete wall
and branches of fir were caught on the rim.
In my mind I recall that asphalt strip
that wound upwards through scented woodruff,
white-tipped nettles, hawkweed, and buttercups.
Then the cylindrical cement tower, then the garden

where we used to see the old English prof., once
the heroine of a work valued by those who know
(a painful, though charming fate). This place
promised us, and you as well, a blessed breach
within reality. It even translated a foreign continent
into a landscape of porches and doors – almost our own.

Here, beside a multi-sided city of little hope,
where you can't even feel your friends dissolve,
we experienced the usual durations of time –
the blue March clearings above steep cliffs,
an August oppressed by sodden shadows,
and the formidable flames of early November.

Here, two or three guests stood for a multitude.
Here, we gathered at the table, sipping Hendrick's gin,
gazing at the pictures from another century, and the black
piano loomed in the room. Here, on a bench, we joked
about how there must be an empyrean of language
where purified forms live on through the years –

like the vocative and aorist. That's where,
when this world is done, you'll continue to hull
the verbal mysteries. But language is not all.
We knew you did not like so much to recall
the wagon, the winter of war, or the Kotlas frost
where you fell into formations of prisoner's threads.

But from that time, habits remained – you knew
how to properly clutch a saw, trim a tree.
That learning lived on in your nerves and sinews
even when, as you put it one day, you began the slide
into darkness – each time a steeper surface,
from ward to ward, from coma to coma.

A goldfinch flutters within a greening bush,
or perhaps an oriole. A new season ripens
and clover caps redden on the lawn.
The world has changed, but you will not,
leaning on the armchair's back like when
you listened to Bach that time before last.

Substance does not die, say the theologians.
Or maybe it's just memory and forgiveness
that remain. We don't know another universe.
This one should be enough. Let the fog
of photographs console, the four elements,
the hardly visible sign on the table of a glass.

[RU]

Hurricane

For now, it's just this greenish flashing on the screen.
A spiral turns and twitches. 'This has become the norm.'
It will reach us, perhaps, the day after next.

The skyscraper will sway like an airplane crossing the continent's edge,
dead rats will float above flooded subway platforms,
the car alarm will sound, then subside, like a wounded man,
and airports will not have enough cots for sleeping.

Some will lose their lives – we don't yet know their names.

The suburban family, while grocery stores still work,
purchases cereal. The husband
wanted to evacuate farther from shore, but not the wife.
It's not clear if it's safer in the basement or on the second floor
(the oak's roots are still shallow, so it could crash through the roof).
The children shouldn't hear this argument.
And, for that matter, they don't: they're petting the dog,
reading *Spiderman* to each other,
content that school is out, playing
hide and seek in the convenient dark,
and it's fun to scare the adults
by jumping out of the hallway with a flashlight,
all before a cosy night spent in a sleeping bag.

In the end, children don't behave differently
even when the family must weigh whether to cross borders or stay –
nobody is waiting for them elsewhere, and the chaos at home
might well come to a close. Usually, those arguments
are too late, for the door is already being rattled
by thin young men with lightning bolts on their uniforms,
or a threshing line of soldiers with green tunics sweeps
through the farmstead, or freedom fighters hurry
to off collaborators, or a mob with machetes approaches.
The human being, as we know, is the only creature
on earth with the wisdom to be mightier
than the elements. For only he knows how
to distinguish dialects and the shapes of skulls,
to determine who belongs to the wrong clan, class
or nation – who's game is up.
It grows light outside the window (the peony blooms, the oriole sings)
because the weather is always good for those who win.

At long last, it's good for us. The flicker on the screen
slides off to the north. A telephone booth, uprooted
from its foundations, lies on the sidewalk,
and the boardwalk has but one lamp left.
Yet the ground steams with warmth. The dog
races with the kids. The trees stand firm. The world
remains the same as it ever was.

[RU]

Three O'Clock at Night on the Sea

In memory of Regina Derieva

The cabin's bulkhead echoed in the dark,
just barely matching the engine's beat.
I groped for the key by my bunk
and entered the corridor half-asleep.
Chain-links, spotlight, tilting steps:
the abyss yawned up ahead.

I didn't understand: why this water, why this sky?
Puddles sloshed and rolled on deck,
my footwear soaked, metal pipes seared,
a loose line waved like a blindworm in its lair –
its scales hardly scraping – the smokestack
colossus murmured through my sleep.

Are we sailing to harbour? Is there a port?
Is this still a ship or only a dangerous risk?
I hovered above the flood's whirling swirls,
feeling like Noah. Deep beneath the swell
tangled roadways appeared, a fortress,
a grove of graves: all in the tempest's grip.

A lighthouse flickered on the horizon
barely caressing Nereus' hair. Space
shimmered like a wind-blown waste
or glass in which no reflection shone.
Gusts blew scatterings of spume
as crest was exchanged for trough.

I slowly deduced what night knew,
what the zodiac carved into salt.
Virtually blinded by slivers of fog,
I could only sense through the cells
of my cheeks how an unseen island hid,
there, by my side, as large as death –

bereft of light. A heavy, blackening star
drawing ephemeral being into its embrace:
deciduous fear, the cascade of a creek,
a wild bay of gneiss and nothingness,
and sandy dunes where a viper leaves
its tracks and the ant always runs late.

Tresses of ivy entwined over stone.
Bats shrieked, hanging from the cavern
walls. Their naked life was sheltered
by a double dark: the cave-like grave
in the hill's crook, and the courage of waves
for which there is no measure.

The island seemed to swim close by:
I recognised it like a blow from behind.
It was that which I cannot experience,
that to which sensation bends, what frightens
imagination because its outline and contents
cannot be repeated, except, perhaps, by silence.

But silence ends and there remains the word.
That's how the body in its den recalls
its speech – on the fourth day, leaning on a wall –
still not knowing if it has understood the ukase.
That is how a patient wave in uninhabited space
hollows out the shore.

[RU]

Syllabic Stanzas

Traveller, your life has finally fulfilled your fate.
Above the pine forest, a star rises from its den,
lack-lustre and dreamy. The density of towers
closes up the shadowed valley, like you: constructed
from consciousness and nothingness, from flame and from clay,
timeless like a well, a hoary plantain, or a rose.
Some gravel, kicked by your foot, scatters against the wall
where twining alleys and gutter knots spool in circles –
a world that has wasted its worth, a world that once fit
between eroding banks and the bus shelter's borders:

an expanse of ancient guilts and older limestone where
a poverty of neon freezes the rancid air –
an expanse conjured into a key, rusting in one's
pocket, into the damp ether's hum, into suppressed
desire, growing more distant than Saturn, rarely dreamed;
nevertheless, you could walk through that space with your eyes
closed (in the wasteland of day, even better at night),
and you could develop a humane dictionary
from its whimsical winds, from its vineyards of voices,
from the lashing rain and arches of Alumnat Yard.

You only talked about this world. The radar of God
would flash with a confusion of crosses. You were not
able to go astray. To the questioner you might
have answered: 'Not on this earth.' You knew bile, treachery,
the unexpected endurance of hopelessness, war
with former friends, grim rows of gravestones, doorways nailed up
diagonally with boards – the cost of returning to
Ithaca. You followed its fall (which you could not hear)
into the abyss of mould. You could easily not
have been, but here you are. The rhythm reborn, breaks down,

the vault splits and crumbles, mirrors crack so that beyond
them you might finally see the place with no glimmer
of hope. Above the stream of time, a blackish leaf drops.
Maybe twenty others already float, each falling
deftly into their essence: reflection and silence.
Bricks have grown rooted and porous, rough to finger's touch.
The fissure in the wall shines white – becoming a star.
There is just this sandy, rain-pierced, and meandering
range of provincial hills, much like the local baroque
you always see – when you imagine death or heaven.

[RU]

The Moss of Ammassalik

You can scarcely read nature's alphabet –
A small cursive script along cliff heights.
Your palm contains just dust and burr:
Whether living or dead, you can't discern.
Wiry forms tangle above the soft cupola –
Maybe willowherb, maybe campanula.

Beyond the ridge spreads a landfill,
A helicopter pad, nondescript huts.
Further – a purposeless land full
Of space, a wasteland. Purling ducts,
Three sea-soaked Matterhorns, a patch
Of hoarfrost by an angular church.

Fog above a boat. Brash ice on the bay.
You will continue here unknown, out of sight.
Nameless crosses in the field have no say,
And no light stays lit throughout the night.
The caravan near Kulusuk was thwarted
By icebergs and has failed to make port.

Grey cataracts make this limbo sing.
A few miles remain to the glacial shield,
While on the cracking granite there clings
The indigenous ashen Yggdrasil.
Its fragile foam covers the vast sprawl,
Though it could just as well not be at all –

No seeds, no roots. A hermaphrodite
That knew love as snow began melting,
It raises its colourless sporophytes
And weighs exactly as much as nothing.
Spreading its crumbling train, it will cover
Rome, Carthage and Leif the Conqueror.

A toothed hill and a boggy coast
Unite the diaphanous body
Which like old tribes is an uncowed host
Ruling the land, a wandering starveling
Whose indifferent fingers will dry
And turn to stones, but never die.

Gently pushing aside a bit of lichen,
Nothing more than the runt of vegetation,
I see the world's peacemaker – twisted
Into the gap between gneiss and mist –
The equal of time, whose essence is fullness
Here where the vault is pierced by loneliness.

The rigging of the Arctic Circle's mien,
The patient green and blue of non-being:
To these mosses you are a passing scene,
Or more precisely, the scenery's state of being.
A shadow passing like doldrums, or a storm
Dissolving into space, the fate of all forms.

[RU]

'Leaving the subway with a pack on my back'
(for E.K.)

Leaving the subway with a pack on my back,
I catch the mixed scent of refuse and seaweed.
Water laps the distant side of the colonnade.
Before – there was no sphinx on the quay,
Thank God for that. Back then, in my youth,
I imbibed those mists every morning.
A physicist lived here. Later,
He moved to the suburbs up north
(More than an hour's bumpy ride on a tramway).
A poet often visited him:
Poems, the news from prison,
Dirty dishes, the tinkle of glassware.
In the old flat, under a dusty lamp,
I sometimes waited for a beauty to arrive.

Look at the photograph. A heath-covered
Hill on the isthmus where swift river rapids
Rinse bunkers. Homeless skerries
Of Finnish granite huddle near shore.
A city spreads across the horizon,
Condemned to death, as Akhmatova said.
An underwater staircase leads into Neptune's
Realm. A country we don't know how to imagine
Sketches itself beyond the tower.
We already sense there is not much time.
We return, forcing ourselves to laugh,
And the warm nights of May silently gather
In the well of the high-windowed courtyard.

What do we want? From what deep layer
Of memory does the echo, steeped in emptiness,
Hatch? Out of what substance
Are the threads of our parting wound?
Where will we die? What angel will bring
Invisible life along the road?
Why do cellos, harps and oboes
Float down to us through darkening skies?

Five streets in a knot. I spent those years
Right here. It seems I recognise the spot
Along the fence where a lost cat
Shelters under the frozen crest of a wall.
Rainwater drips from the gutters.
The poplar at the crossroads has grown old.
Night spreads itself out. A damp reflection
Captures the rusty, but still resonant,
Tin roof. The apartment air vent rattles
A hundred paces from the cold canal.
Such is this simple city harmony –
The whiteness of branches, the blackness of stone.
We are not alone. The world turns to smoke.
Fire flickers above the colonnade.

[RU]

The Way to Planty Park, Kraków

The jasmine blooms between tramway stops.

You could have lived and died here, but decided to return to your own baroque, your knotted alleyways, dilapidated courtyards, the duchy along two rivers, and this you probably won't regret.

So then, old age. The bones grow heavy, the senses slowly close their doors, and dimming eyes no longer see the pinnacles in the sky. A long-legged, raven-haired beauty boards the tram – the type you always liked to see. You hear her every utterance, but can't catch the sense of a single phrase.

Colours and scents are out of joint. You see enough to recognise the doors of Austrian Art Nouveau as they slide by. Then the theatre, the crossing of tram tracks, and a straight road until the rectangular square whose concrete is interrupted by freshly planted wraith-like linden trees.

It's time to say goodbye to cathedrals and paintings, as well as to maps and atlases – things you preferred to most books. Goodbye to coffee steam and the suppleness of a beloved cheek.

To tell the truth, you were lucky. You never knew a prison bed or crushing poverty. You were not destroyed by alcohol, though you lived with it, as everyone in your generation did. You avoided spending eight hours a day filling out forms. You found delight in fruit trees and the female body, though those fruit trees grow no more, and the shawls and hats of your girlfriends have long since frayed. You saw what you wanted to see, but didn't believe you would see. You did a thing or two, but most importantly tried to avoid actions which would bring you shame until death, or even after. You almost succeeded.

You hurt those who loved you, and they forgave you, though you didn't always forgive yourself.

You understood that it's wrong to march in step with the crowd – even when, or especially when, the hymn they sing is easily understood and your own.

Your poems will be read by one or two people at night, but thank God, never recited at a government event.

You walked on the edge of the abyss – specialists gave it the Latin name, *id* – but you were able to keep it at bay. The alarm clock helped, stirring you to work each morning, but really it was the declensions and prosody of words.

As Solon warned, it can all fall apart. Call no man happy until he's lived through all his appointed days. And there are thousands of those days, not a single one like another.

But the angel that watched over you since childhood, on the slopes of the Nemunas and in suburban alleys under silver spruce, will probably still be with you, as long as you know how to ask.

Everything gets bigger towards the end – distances, jasmine bouquets, and cobblestones. Only wonder has no dimensions, wonder that there is a world at all, and that it remains after you are gone.

[RU]

Variation on the Theme of Awakening

What echoes in the dark? Is it the wind of June
in the gardens by the lake? If so, the two of us
are in the summer house up high, still young,
having fallen asleep just before dawn.
A muffled engine? Then we're in that dive
by the harbour, in a country where we'd prefer
not to linger, worn out, not by love, but by the journey
over a wind-swept bay. Or maybe it's the chirping
of a decrepit, old-fashioned alarm clock
ineptly penetrating the parching air?
If so, then I know I've awakened in Tuscany,
but the name of the town escapes me.

The times are in a knot. Impossible to unravel
the nuances of years, places, sounds. A hand
remains, still pressed against my palm, and
a gentle sigh marking the passage of a dream
is more easily understood than one's voice.
What has melded together will not melt apart.
Our children have grown and left us alone.
So many friends have passed away. Almost everyday,
faces float up from a fog of photographs –
faces we'll never see again on this earth.
And in the concert hall, flanked by urban maples,
the doors of night are opened by draughts of sound.

The curtain sways. Beyond the window shutters
foliage fades into dim murmuration
while limpid silhouettes climb the walls.
By now it doesn't matter if this is called
love, or incorrigible fidelity: we share
a fathomless fear, as when the plane
carrying you home is late, or when
bloody traces stain the cotton pad
you try to hide from my sight.
Let's go to sleep. Let's imagine we don't know
that one of us will be the first to go.
Better to vanish, than to be left alone.

An echo once more. Clarifying to a bell.
From a church? A clock-tower? All the same.
From longing, disagreements, pain
a world is born belonging to two
which is shared like a gift
while the unknown beats its wings above.
We were fated to prune grape vines,
to build a roof from Lebanese cedar,
and to burn in undying flame.
It's almost dawn. As ordered in the Book,
I will not wake you till you please.
I listen to the bell, my breath held tight.

[RU]

Delft

When futile pain and retribution are all that's left,
And time breaks both guilty and innocent without regret,
You and I will depart forever – and go to Delft.

To the delta: to green canals, to the multicellular
Facades on the embankment. Well, check the door –
So we can remain undiscovered – evermore.

The neighbour is discreet; his plate screwed tight.
The lens has been wiped clear: the slide is bright –
Leeuwenhoek laughs as he strains his sight.

The eye is key: blinks open – blue and yellow.
A roof above the wall, rough river sand below.
The pearl under the temple, or just a shadow.

The State's indifferent. Fate is lax, powerless.
The search for honour futile; we won't amass riches,
It's just good to know there are those thirty-four canvases.

Like life, they exist – but no meaning bestow.
The girl reads the letter at the open window.
Written by us – another? No one will ever know.

[EH]

To My Daughter

We separated twice, and you grew up.
These are your gifts: a southern way of being,
Brown eyes, flickering shyly, and a gait
That one could easily mistake for flying.
It was not I who left those traits, but rather
Generations we were not fated to see,
Though they are with us still – like a coastal whirlwind,
A treetop through the pane, a play of light,
A pine cone at the cemetery gate.
We say goodbye again and then repeat,
For rupture is the only fact of life.

Two segments overlapped for just a moment,
And in the empty spaces still ahead,
I too will be the twilight through the foliage,
A contour glowing in the dust and wind.
We're losing the connection. The air is stunned,
The shining day, pointless and unmoving.
Souls amble through the thicket of the heavens,
And again the offspring differs from the parents.
Listen. In the labyrinths of that epoch,
I will have become a light footprint, embedded in
My language, which you only know in fragments.

[DS]

'Let the time you no longer remember'

Let the time you no longer remember,
and the world you have not yet found,
be as black and white as stones are –
as the names of apple trees and boulevards.

Let there be sugar, cheese and allotted
in glasses: rough, bevelled water.
In movie theatres let the lights go out,
and let nightingales in junkyard lots
argue their cases for many hours.

Let gunpowder's aftertaste remind you
that dawn has only just begun to rise,
that provincial trains are passing through
the great menageries of cities –

For the canal, in which a tear pulsates,
has been ever so lightly traced
with pencil lead and yellow salt –
by the hand of an unfathomable God.

[EH]

APPENDICES

NOTES

On Both Sides of Alnas Lake (25):
Alnas (Holny) is a lake in northern Poland, close to the Lithuanian border. As a young man, Czesław Miłosz used to swim across it.

To Master Radovan (27):
Radovan, an eighteenth-century artist, sculpted the portal of the Cathedral of St Lawrence in Trogir, Dalmatia. He shares a first name with Radovan Karadžić, a contemporary Bosnian Serb politician and convicted war criminal.

Dictator (29):
The dictator evoked in this poem is Romania's Nicolae Ceaușescu, who was executed in 1989.

The Process of Beatification (31):
According to a legend, Russian émigré nun Elizaveta Kuzmina-Karavaeva (Mother Maria, 1891–1945) saved a female French Resistance fighter by exchanging clothes with her, allowing her to escape from prison.

Azovstal (34):
The poem's penultimate stanza quotes a line by Russian poet Vladimir Pecherin (1807–85).

The Grove of the Eumenides (39):
This poem alludes to Sophocles's *Oedipus at Colonus*. Today, Colonus (Kolonos) is a disadvantaged suburb of Athens.

Landscape with Polyphemus (54):
This poem takes its title from the painting by Nicholas Poussin.

Prehistory (58):

Klaipėda (Memel) is the city where Tomas Venclova was born just before World War II. Memel was mainly German-speaking at the time. Marinesco was a Soviet submarine captain who in 1945 ordered the sinking of the ship *Wilhelm Gustloff*, which was carrying thousands of refugees.

Cavalryman near Seinai (60):

The cavalryman evoked here is Nikolai Gumilev (1886-1921), Russian poet and husband of Anna Akhmatova. He fought near the town of Seinai (Sejny) during World War I. Akhmatova prayed for him at Ostra Brama (Aušros Vartai, the 'Gate of Dawn' chapel in Vilnius). He was never wounded on the battlefield, but was executed after the war by the Bolsheviks.

'It's not instantly clear why it comes up so rich' (79):

This poem evokes the author's childhood in Kaunas in the early postwar years (1946–47). Many of Kaunas's toponyms are mentioned.

Hamden, Connecticut (87):

This poem is partly patterned after 'North Haven' by Elizabeth Bishop. The deceased friend mentioned is Alexander Schenker, a Yale professor who in his youth was imprisoned in Siberia.

Syllabic Stanzas (94):

The poem's last lines paraphrase W.H. Auden's 'In Praise of Limestone'.

The Moss of Ammassalik (96):

Tasiilaq (Ammassalik island) is a small town in southeastern Greenland.

The Way to Planty Park, Kraków (100):

The Planty is the garden ring in central Kraków, Poland.

Variation on the Theme of Awakening (102):

The opening lines of the poem refer to 'In Limbo' by Richard Wilbur, hence, the word 'variation' in the title.

SOURCES FOR POEMS

UOB   *Už Onos ir Bernardinų* (Beyond St Anne's and the Bernardines)
Apostrofa, Vilnius, 2023.

EG   *Eumenidžių giraitė* (The Grove of the Eumenides)
Versus Aureus, Vilnius, 2016.

Visi   *Visi Eilėrašciai* (Collected Poems)
Lietuvių Literatūros ir Tautosakos Institutas, Vilnius, 2010.

On Both Sides of Alnas Lake / UOB
To Master Radovan / Visi
Dictator / Visi
The Process of Beatification / EG
Before the Fort / UOB
Azovstal / UOB
Flight / EG
The Grove of the Eumenides / EG
South of the Prospect / EG
Chinese Impressions / Visi
Landscape with Polyphemus / UOB
Three Imperfect Sonnets / Visi
'The stream of smoke dissolved...' / EG
Prehistory / Visi
Cavalryman near Seinai / EG
Beyond St Anne's and the Bernardines / UOB
Extra Urbem / EG
Caligula at the Gates / EG
August Elegy / EG
Notes of Xenophon / EG
Death of the Argonaut / UOB

'Tell me, what did you love? One city you left behind' / EG
Mother of the Living / EG
'It's not instantly clear why it comes up so rich' / UOB
From the Future / UOB
Kotor Sun / UOB
Eos / UOB
Hamden, Connecticut / UOB
Hurricane / EG
Three O'Clock at Night on the Sea / EG
Syllabic Stanzas / Visi
The Moss of Ammassalik / EG
'Leaving the subway with a pack on my back' / UOB
The Way to Planty Park, Kraków / UOB
Variation on the Theme of Awakening / Visi
Delft / UOB
To My Daughter / UOB
'Let the time you no longer remember' / Visi

TOMAS VENCLOVA: SELECTED BIBLIOGRAPHY

WORKS IN ENGLISH

The Grove of the Eumenides: New & Selected Poems, ed. Ellen Hinsey, tr. Ellen Hinsey, Diana Senechal and Rimas Užgiris (Hexham: Bloodaxe Books, 2025).

Magnetic North: Conversations with Tomas Venclova and Ellen Hinsey (Rochester: Rochester University Press/UK edition: Boydell and Brewer, 2017).

Vilnius: A Personal History (Riverdale-on-Hudson: Sheep Meadow Press, 2009).

The Junction: Selected Poems, ed. Ellen Hinsey, tr. Ellen Hinsey, Constantine Rusanov and Diana Senechal (Tarset: Bloodaxe Books, 2008).

Tomas Venclova (Poems), tr. Laima Sruoginis (Klaipėda: House of Artists, 2002).

Vilnius, tr. Aušra Simanavičiūtė (Vilnius: R. Paknio leidykla, 2001).

Forms of Hope (Essays), (Riverdale-on-Hudson: Sheep Meadow Press, 1999).

Winter Dialogue, tr. Diana Senechal (Evanston, Ill.: Northwestern University Press, 1997).

Aleksander Wat: Life and Art of an Iconoclast (New Haven and London: Yale University Press, 1996).

Lithuanian Literature, tr. Algirdas Landsbergis (New York: Lithuanian National Foundation, Inc., 1979).

SELECTED WORKS IN LITHUANIAN

Lietuvos istorija visiems, II tomas (A History of Lithuania, vol. II), Vilnius: R. Paknio leidykla, 2019.

Lietuvos istorija visiems, I tomas (A History of Lithuania, vol. I), Vilnius: R. Paknio leidykla, 2018.

Eumenidžių giraitė (The Grove of the Eumenides, poems), Vilnius: Versus Aureus, 2016.

Prarasto orumo beieškant: publicistikos straipsnių rinktinė (In Search of Lost Dignity, essays), Vilnius: Lietuvos nacionalinė Martyno Mažvydo biblioteka, 2016.

Pertrūkis tikrovėje (A Break in Reality, essays), Vilnius, 2013.

Vilnius: asmeninė istorija (Vilnius: A Personal History), Vilnius: R. Paknio leidykla, 2011.

Visi eilėraščiai: 1956-2010 (Collected Poems), Vilnius: Lietuvių literatūros ir tautosakos institutas, 2010.

Kitaip: poezijos vertimu rinktine (Otherwise, selected translations), Vilnius: Lietuvos rašytojų sąjungos leidykla, 2006.

Vilniaus vardai (People from Vilnius), Vilnius: R. Paknio leidykla, 2006.

Sankirta: Eilėraščiai (The Junction, poetry), Vilnius: Lietuvos rašytojų sąjungos leidykla, 2005.

Ligi Lietuvos 10 000 kilometrų (10,000 Kilometres to Lithuania, journal), Vilnius: Baltos lankos, 2003.

Vilnius: Vadovas po miestą (Vilnius City Guide), Vilnius: R. Paknio leidykla, 2001.

Manau, kad... Pokalbiai su Tomu Venclova (I think that... Interviews with Tomas Venclova), Vilnius: Baltos lankos, 2000.

Rinktinė (Selected Poems), Vilnius: Baltos lankos, 1999.

Reginys iš alėjos: eilėraščiai (A View from an Alley, poetry), Vilnius: Baltos lankos, 1998.

Pašnekesys žiemą: eilėraščiai ir vertimai (Winter Dialogue, poetry), Vilnius: Vaga, 1991.

Vilties formos: eseistika ir publicistika (Forms of Hope, essays), Vilnius: Lietuvos rašytojų sąjungos leidykla, 1991.

Tankėjanti šviesa: eilėraščiai (The Condensing Light, poetry), Chicago: Algimanto Mackaus knygų leidimo fondas, 1990.

Tekstai apie tekstus (Texts on Texts, essays), Chicago: Algimanto Mackaus knygų leidimo fondas, 1985.

Lietuva pasaulyje (Lithuania in the World, essays), Chicago: Akademinės skautijos leidykla, 1981.

98 eilėraščiai (98 Poems, poetry), Chicago: Algimanto Mackaus knygų leidimo fondas, 1977.

Kalbos ženklas (The Sign of Speech, poetry), Vilnius: Vaga, 1972.

Golemas, arba dirbtinis žmogus: pokalbiai apie kibernetiką (The Golem or Artificial Man: Discussions on Cybernetics), Vilnius, 1965.

Raketos, planetos ir mes (Rockets, Planets and Us), Vilnius: Valstybinė grožinės literatūros leidykla, 1962.

WORKS WRITTEN IN RUSSIAN

Собеседники на пиру: Литературные эссе (Participants at a Feast: Literary Essays), Москва, НЛО, 2012.

Статьи о Бродском (Studies on Brodsky), Москва: Baltrus, Новое издательство, 2005.

Собеседники на пиру: Статьи о русской литературе (Participants at a Feast: Studies on Russian Literature), Vilnius: Baltos lankos, 1997.

Неустойчивое равновесие: восемь русских поэтических текстов (The Unstable Equilibrium: Eight Russian Poetic Texts), New Haven: YCIAS, 1986.

OTHER EDITIONS

Czesław Miłosz, Tomas Venclova, Powroty do Litwy (Returns to Lithuania) (poems, correspondence and essays), Warsaw: Zeszyty Literackie, 2011.

Пограничье: Публицистика разных лет (Borderland: Political Essays from Various Years), Санкт-Петербург: Издательство Ивана Лимбаха, 2015.

THE TRANSLATORS

Ellen Hinsey is the author of nine books of poetry, essays, dialogue and literary translation, with a focus on Eastern Europe and democracy. Her volumes of poetry include *The Invisible Fugue* (Wildhouse Poetry, 2024); *The Illegal Age* (Arc Publications, 2017), a Poetry Book Society Choice; *Update on the Descent* (Bloodaxe Books, 2009), a National Poetry Series Finalist in the US, written after her experiences at the International Criminal Tribunal for the Former Yugoslavia in the Hague; *The White Fire of Time* (Wesleyan University Press, US, 2002, Bloodaxe Books, UK, 2003), and *Cities of Memory* (Yale University Press, 1995), which received the Yale University Series Award. Her essays are collected in *Mastering the Past: Contemporary Central and Eastern Europe and the Rise of Illiberalism* (2017). Her book-length dialogue with Tomas Venclova, *Magnetic North*, explores post-war culture and ethics under totalitarianism and was a finalist for Lithuania's Book of the Year. Hinsey also edited and co-translated Tomas Venclova's *The Junction: Selected Poems* (2008). Her work has appeared in publications such as *The New York Times*, *The New Yorker*, *The Irish Times*, *Frankfurter Allgemeine Zeitung*, *Paris Review* and *Poetry*. Her book-length translations of contemporary French literature include *The Secret Piano: From Mao's Labor Camps to Bach's Goldberg Variations* by Zhu Xiao-Mei. A former Berlin Prize Fellow of the American Academy in Berlin and a DAAD Künstlerprogramm Fellow, she has been the recipient of Lannan and Rona Jaffe Foundation Awards, among others. She has most recently been a visiting professor at Göttingen University.

Diana Senechal was born in Tucson and holds a PhD in Slavic languages and literatures from Yale University. She is the 2011 winner of the Hiett Prize in the Humanities and the author of the volume of poetry *Solo Concert* (Serving House Books, 2025) as well as two books of nonfiction from Rowman & Littlefield, Republic of Noise (2011) and Mind over Memes (2018), as well as numerous poems, stories, essays, and translations. Her translation of Gyula Jenei's *Mindig más* (Always Different: Poems of Memory) was published in 2022 by Deep Vellum. Her work has appeared in publications such as *The New York Review of Books, The Partisan Review, Orient Express, 2B: A Journal of Ideas* and *Metamorphosis*. Her earlier translations of Tomas Venclova's poems are featured in *The Junction* (2008) and her selected translations of Tomas Venclova, *Winter Dialogue*, appeared with Northwestern University Press in 1997. She has also translated selections by Anna Akhmatova, Bella Akhmadulina, Marina Tsvetaeva and Aleksandr Kushner. She has been an invited participant at the International Miłosz Festival and PEN International. Her poetry and fiction have appeared in numerous publications. Her teaching and performance work has been featured in *The New York Times*. She has been living in Hungary since 2017.

Rimas Užgiris is a poet, translator, editor and critic. His work has appeared in *Barrow Street, AGNI, Atlanta Review, Iowa Review, Quiddity, Hudson Review, Vilnius Review* and other journals. He is translation editor and primary translator of *How the Earth Carries Us: New Lithuanian Poets*, and translator of *Caravan Lullabies* by Ilzė Butkutė (2016), Vagabond Sun by Judita Vaičiūnaitė (2018), and *Then What: Selected Poems* by Gintaras Grajauskas (Bloodaxe Books, 2018). He holds a PhD in philosophy from the University of Wisconsin-Madison and an MFA in creative writing from Rutgers-Newark University and teaches translation at Vilnius University. He has received a Fulbright Scholar Grant, a National Endowment for the Arts Literature Translation Fellowship, and the Poetry Spring 2016 Award for his translations of Lithuanian poetry into other languages.

EU DECLARATION OF GPSR CONFORMITY

Books published by Bloodaxe Books are identified by the EAN/ISBN printed above our address on the copyright page and manufactured by the printer whose address is noted below. This declaration of conformity is issued under the sole responsibility of the publisher, the object of declaration being each individual book produced in conformity with the relevant EU harmonisation legislation with no known hazards or warnings, and is made on behalf of Bloodaxe Books Ltd on 20 November 2025 by Neil Astley, Managing Director, editor@bloodaxebooks.com.

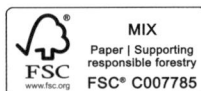

MIX
Paper | Supporting
responsible forestry
FSC
www.fsc.org
FSC® C007785